North Florida Waterways

by

Kevin McCarthy

Some residents of our North Florida waterways

Nature Coast Publishing House

2013

Copyright © 2013 Kevin McCarthy

All rights reserved.

ISBN - 13: 978-1492270386
ISBN - 10: 1492270385

The image on the cover is of Wekiva Springs
south of Ocala and north of Orlando.

The image on the title page is of
a gator and some turtles on one of our rivers.

Also by Kevin McCarthy

Grammar and Usage (1980)
Saudi Arabia: A Desert Kingdom (1986)
The History of Gilchrist County (1986)
The AVT Learning System in Writing: Grammar
 and Paragraphs (1986)
Alligator Tales (1988)
Florida Lighthouses (1990)
Thirty Florida Shipwrecks (1992)
The Book Lover's Guide to Florida (1992)
African Americans in Florida (1993)
The Gators and the Seminoles (1993)
Twenty Florida Pirates (1994)
The Hippocrene U.S.A. Guide to Black Florida (1995)
Baseball in Florida (1996)
Twentieth-Century Florida Authors (1996)
Lighthouses of Ireland (1997)
Guide to UF and Gainesville (1997)
Georgia's Lighthouses & Historic Coastal Sites (1998)
Native Americans in Florida (1999)
Fightin' Gators: A History of University of Florida Football
 (2000)
Christmas in Florida (2000)
Ocala (2001)
Florida Outhouses (2002)
Babe Ruth in Florida (2002)
African Americans at the University of Florida (2003)
Honoring the Past, Shaping the Future: The University
 of Florida, 1853-2003 (2003)

(continued on next page)

Aviation in Florida (2003)
Women at the University of Florida (2004)
Apalachicola Bay (2004)
Greek Americans of Florida (2004)
St. Johns River Guidebook (2004)
Over Southeast Florida (2005)
Cedar Key, Florida: A History (2007)
African American Sites in Florida (2007)
Benjamin Otis Franklin Jr.: His Life Story (2008)
Turkey 2 Volunteers in the Peace Corps: 1963 – 2008 (2008)
Micanopy: An Illustrated History (2008)
Suwannee River Guidebook (2009)
Historic Photos of University of Florida Football (2009)
Lake City, Florida: A Sesquicentennial Tribute (2009)
Judge Stephan P. Mickle: His Life and Legacy (2010)
Carl Joseph: Some Called Me "Superstar" (2010)
Remembering University of Florida Football (2011)
Hillsborough River Guidebook (2011)
The Marjorie Kinnan Rawlings Society: The First 25 Years
    (2012)
Caloosahatchee River Guidebook (2012)
Lincoln High School: Its History and Legacy (2012)
Castles of Turkey (2013)

Plus 9 edited collections of stories by others

Table of Contents

Introduction i

I: Rivers 1
Chapter 1: How Rivers Formed Florida's Borders .. 3

St. Johns River: introduction 5
Chapter 2: The Sinking of the *America* Yacht 7
Chapter 3: Fort Gates Ferry 11

Suwannee River: introduction 15
Chapter 4: Florida's Official Song 17
Chapter 5: The Ghost Town of Columbus 21

Apalachicola River: introduction 25
Chapter 6: Harvesting Oysters in Apalachicola Bay 27

Chapter 7: Ferries on North Florida Rivers 31

Chapter 8: Boating Parties on North Florida Rivers 35

II: Lakes in North Florida 39
Chapter 9: Indian Canoes in Newnans Lake 41
Chapter 10: Lake Harris 45

III: Springs in North Florida 49
Chapter 11: Hart Springs 51
Chapter 12: Wakulla Springs 55

IV: Shipwrecks in North Florida 59
Chapter 13: *Maple Leaf* 61
Chapter 14: *City of Hawkinsville* 65
Chapter 15: *Commodore* 69

continued on next page

V: Watery Critters 73
Chapter 16: Birds That Also Fish in North Florida 75
Chapter 17: Loggerhead Turtles 79
Chapter 18: Ugly North Florida Fish 83
Chapter 19: The Many Fish Species of North Florida's Waters
.... 87
Conclusion 91
Bibliography 91
Photo credits 92
About the author 93
Index 94

Some fishermen on the Suwannee River

Introduction

This collection of essays offers vignettes of the waterways of North Florida: the rivers, lakes, rivers, springs, Atlantic Ocean, and Gulf of Mexico, the latter two as they relate to this part of the state.

Some of these essays began as my contributions to a wonderful asset available for free to anglers and boaters around the country: *Coastal Angler Magazine*, especially its north-central Florida edition. I especially want to acknowledge the good work by that edition's co-editors: Lynn and Cary Crutchfield. For online versions of each month's issue, see this web site: http://coastalanglermag.com/local-editions/.

I want to particularly thank my wife, Karelisa Hartigan, for her editing of the manuscript and for her companionship on many of my trips to and on our Florida waterways.

I: Rivers of North Florida: Introduction

One of the state's greatest assets is its waterways. A major component of that asset is the river. Florida has some 150 rivers, ranging from the long and large (St. Johns, Suwannee) to the short and small (Miami, various Dead Rivers).

Some of the rivers begin out of state (Apalachicola, Suwannee), while others begin in Florida's swamps. I had the privilege of boating almost the entire length of four of the rivers (St. Johns, Suwannee, Hillsborough, Caloosahatchee) and writing guidebooks about them.

These rivers have been here for thousands of years. Native Americans lived along them, boated and fished them, and shared them with mammoths and mastodons. In the 19th century, the rivers allowed new residents to travel to new sites by all kinds of boats. Soldiers and sailors used the rivers to seek out the enemy and even sink the vessels of opposing forces. Some of those sunken boats, well preserved if they sank into the airless muck, have been found and searched for artifacts from the past.

The Apalachicola River near Torreya State Park

Rivers

This part of the book discusses how rivers determined our borders and then describes parts of three rivers in North Florida: the St. Johns (how the *America* yacht was deliberately sunk in the river; the Fort Gates Ferry), the Suwannee (how Stephen Foster wrote our official state song; the ghost town at Columbus along the river); and the Apalachicola (harvesting oysters in Apalachicola Bay).

St. Marks River near Tallahassee is one of the many beautiful rivers in North Florida.

Some of our rivers inspired writers, including British poet Samuel Taylor Coleridge. The so-called disappearance of the Ichetucknee for several miles underground amazed naturalist William Bartram, whose description led Coleridge to write "Kubla Khan." Another river, the Suwannee, helped determine East Florida from West Florida. So now let's take a closer look at three of our rivers.

Chapter 1: How Rivers Formed Florida's Borders

While Florida's eastern, southern, and western borders are clear (the Atlantic Ocean and the Gulf of Mexico), rivers played a major part in determining her northern border. Those rivers can, in fact, help explain why that border is not simply a straight line from the Atlantic to the Perdido River, why in fact it looks so strange at the eastern end and middle of that border.

The original northern border of Florida, as claimed by the Spanish, was up at the Savannah River, which today forms the boundary between Georgia and South Carolina. When Georgia's colonists defeated Spanish forces in the 1739 Battle of Bloody Marsh on St. Simons Island, Spain was forced to retreat and admit that the north-eastern border of Florida was not the Savannah River, but in fact was the St. Marys River (see the map to the left).

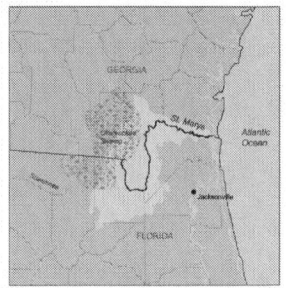

That was fine except that the St. Marys dramatically changes directions about thirty miles (48 km) from the sea, heading due south for about thirty miles (48 km), then jogging to the west and then to the north. At that point the border heads due west, cutting through the Okefenokee Swamp over to the town of Chattahoochee and Lake Seminole.

A steamboat on the St. Marys River

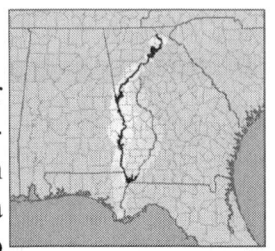

Rivers

From Lake Seminole, the border heads north along the Chattahoochee River (see map to the right), which joins with the Flint River to form the Apalachicola River, which flows through Florida into the Gulf of Mexico. After going north for about twenty miles (32 km) along the Chattahoochee, the border goes due west, following the 31st parallel. That line was established in 1663, when a royal charter created the Carolina Colony, some 70 years before Georgia was established.

Florida's western border used to be the Mississippi River, but that changed in 1810, when American troops took over part of West Florida from the Pearl River to the Mississippi. Three years later, because Spain supported the British in the War of 1812, American forces seized more land over to the Perdido River. That action gave America Mobile Bay and an important port near the Gulf of Mexico. The name of the river goes back to Spanish *perdido* meaning "lost" for reasons unknown.

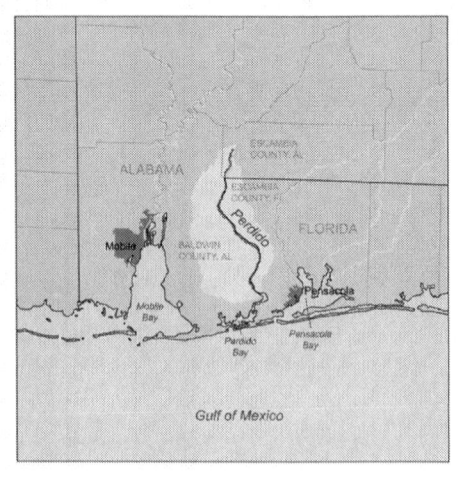

So this is why the state's northern border is so strange and how rivers played a major role in determining that border.

Some people still think that Florida should extend all the way to the Mississippi River, but that's an argument for another day.

St. Johns River

Introduction to the River

At a length of 310 miles (500 km), the St. Johns River is the longest river in Florida (see map to the left). It goes through or borders 12 counties and is one of the few rivers in the United States that flows north. It flows rather slowly from its source in Indian River County. It has been important in the history of the state as many residents traveled up it to settle along the river long before roads were built.

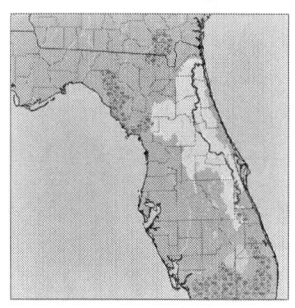

In 1998, the U.S. Environmental Protection Agency named the waterway one of this country's American Heritage Rivers because of its natural, economic, agricultural, scenic, historic, cultural, and recreational resources. Ten years later, the St. Johns had deteriorated so much that it was included on a list of this country's Ten Most Endangered Rivers because of its pollution.

Manatees in Blue Spring State Park on the upper (southern) part of the St. Johns

As the river flows north, several tributaries, like the Wekiva River, feed into it. The St. Johns affects around 4 million people who live within the watersheds that feed into the river. So many people in those watersheds have caused much pollution, but scientists are doing their best to control and/or end that pollution.

The St. Johns River passes Jacksonville before entering the Atlantic Ocean.

The major city along the river is Jacksonville. A short distance further on, the river turns east and enters the Atlantic Ocean at Mayport, which has Naval Station Mayport, the second-largest Atlantic fleet operation in the country.

For several thousand years, dating back to the Native Americans, people have settled along the river, fished its depths, boated its waters, and enjoyed one of the most important waterways in this state. It has seen its share of history and battles, as well as important personages. In and along the river are many species of wildlife, for example the Barred Owl.

This part of the book will discuss two parts of the river: the sinking of a famous yacht and a modern ferry. (Also see Chapter 11 [*Maple Leaf*] for an important shipwreck in the river.)

Chapter 2: The Sinking of the *America* Yacht

One of the tributaries of the St. Johns River is Dunns Creek, which is about 17 miles (27 km) south of Palatka. It leads from the river to Crescent Lake, a freshwater body of water that is almost 16,000 acres (65 square kilometers) in size. How Dunns Creek is connected to what is assuredly the most famous yacht in American history is not generally known.

Dunns Creek today is a tributary of the St. Johns River.

The story began in 1851, when the New York Yacht Club commissioned an architect to design a schooner, which they called *America*. The vessel in final form weighed 170 tons and had a very long bow and tall rig.

When launched, the yacht sailed across the Atlantic to England for a race against British vessels – with the winner taking home something called the Royal Yacht Squadron 100 Guineas Cup, so named for what it cost to make it.

Rivers

The America *was sleek and fast.*

The *America* easily won the 53-mile (85-km) race around the Isle of Wight. Legend has it that Queen Victoria asked those around her who were also watching the race: "Which boat is winning? And which one is next?" The answer to the second question: "Your Majesty, there is no second." The young upstart American entry outstripped her competitors and claimed the trophy, renamed the America's Cup, one that would remain in American hands until 1983.

After the race, the boat's owners sold the vessel to an Englishman. With a change of owners and name, first to *Camilla* and then to *Memphis*, the boat eventually wound up in the American Civil War as a blockade runner for the Confederacy. It carried goods between Nassau, Bermuda, and the southern states.

The America *served on both sides during the Civil War.*

The Sinking of the *America* Yacht

In 1862, with the blockade of Southern ports getting tighter, the *Memphis* entered the St. Johns River and wound up in Jacksonville. When Union troops began approaching that city, Confederate sailors took the *Memphis* up the river to Dunns Creek off the St. Johns River, where they hurriedly sank the vessel in order to keep her out of Union hands.

When Union troops heard about the vessel, they went searching for her, found her in the creek, raised her, renamed her *America*, and made her part of the Union blockade of the South.

She thus served on both sides during the Civil War, which was appropriate since much of the nation had applauded her when she beat the best of the English yachts in 1851.

New owners of the yacht refitted her in the late 1800s, reducing her masts and lengthening her spars. They also added two extra headsails and a fore gaff topsail. The image above shows what the refitted yacht looked like.

A group of yachtsmen later bought and refurbished her, before presenting her to the U.S. Naval Academy in Annapolis as a gift of gratitude for the fame she had brought America in that famous race. There she remained until a blizzard destroyed her in 1942. A strange ending to a really proud vessel!

That sleek yacht stirred patriotic emotions on this side of the Atlantic the way very few boats or ships in our history have ever done. The world's most famous yachting race continues to commemorate this nation's best-known yacht. And little Dunns Creek played a part in that history.

The U.S. Naval Academy was the final resting place of the yacht.

Chapter 3: Fort Gates Ferry

One can cross the St. Johns River by various means; by foot or on a bridge or even swimming, but they don't match the excitement of a ferry boat. The river has several modern-day ferries, for example the large vessels at Mayport or the small pontoon boat to Hontoon Island or a private one to Drayton Island.

The Fort Gates Ferry in the early 1900s

One of the oldest ferries is the Fort Gates Ferry, a public ferry which connects the small town of Fruitland with the Ocala National Forest. Six days a week (it doesn't run on Tuesdays) one can drive west about 7 miles (11 km) from Crescent City on highway 308 or east on National Forest Road 43 off U.S. 19 for about 7.5 miles (12 km) on a dirt road to the river and follow the signs for the ferry.

The ferry in the mid-1900s

The ferry, which operates just north of Lake George, is run by a man who lives on the east side and can be found in a trailer there. If you arrive on the west side of the river, flash your lights and/or call the operator (386-467-2411). The ferry operates from 7:00 a.m. to 5:30 p.m. and costs $10/car and $5/motorcycle.

Rivers

The ferry landing in 1984

The mile-long crossing takes about 10 minutes, depending on the weather and boat traffic. It's been operating since 1854. Confederate soldiers operated it as a military ferry during the Civil War.

This oldest ferry still operating in the state can carry 2 or 3 cars or pickups, a dozen motorcycles, and almost 40 bicycles. It carries about 1500 vehicles a year.

An 18-foot- (5.5-meter-) long tugboat named "Too Wendy" (the operator wasn't sure about why it is called that) pushes the ferry, which can handle up to 15 tons.

The little tugboat was converted from a 1910 Sharpie sailboat. See the picture of the little tugboat to the right.

The tugboat that pushes the ferry

Putnam County partly funds the ferry operation as part of its public transportation service. A 2009 contest promoting a particular brand of motor oil featured the ferry in something called the "World's Worst Commute," but many locals and tourists depend on the service, After all, the short run across the river can save up to 50 miles (80.5 km) of driving up to Palatka and then down one side of the river or the other.

Many people depend on the ferry to get their vehicles across.

The ferry with two motorcycles approaches the dock.

Actor Paul Newman was in a car commercial on the ferry in 1972 and apparently even stayed for dinner with the boat operator.

So, if you're in the area on any day other than Tuesday, try out the ferry.

Cars and motorcycles can easily go onto and off the ferry.

One person can operate the ferry.

Suwannee River

Introduction to the river

One of the best-known rivers in all of Florida is the Suwannee, which flows for about 246 miles (396 km) from southern Georgia through several counties in North Florida to the Gulf of Mexico. (See map to the right.)

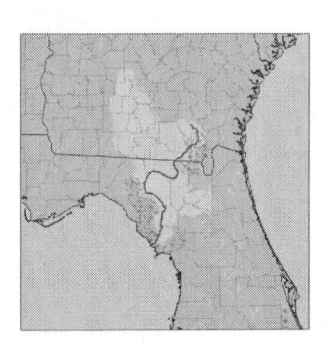

The waterway begins in Georgia's Okefenokee Swamp, goes through Fargo, Georgia, and then winds through Florida. Several rivers, for example the Alapaha, Santa Fe, and Withlacoochee, as well as many major springs, add a huge volume of water to the river.

The upper river can be very peaceful, except during flooding.

Rivers

Boat ramps all along the Suwannee allow visitors to launch their boats into the river.

East of White Springs the river goes through layers of limestone rocks, which cause a very rare phenomenon in Florida: white-water rapids. Unsuspecting boaters (like the author of this work) will be very surprised at the force of the water rushing through the dangerous rocks.

People have inhabited areas along the river for several thousand years, beginning with Native Americans two thousand years ago. Later tribes included the Timucua and then the Seminoles. In the 19th century white settlers moved in, many of them attracted to the beneficial effects of bathing in sulphur springs around White Springs. (Also see Chapter 11 [Hart Springs] and Chapter 14 [*City of Hawkinsville*].)

Bridges over the Suwannee show how high floods have reached.

Chapter 4: Florida's Official Song

The great musical composer Stephen Foster (1826 – 1864) is called the "Father of American Music" because he wrote over 200 songs, many of which became very famous. One of his best-known songs is "Old Folks at Home," which is better known as "The Swanee River" or "Way Down Upon the Suwannee River."

While writing the song in Pittsburgh, Pennsylvania, in 1851, he searched for the name of a Southern river for the opening line of his lyrics.

Two river names that he rejected were Yazoo (for a Mississippi river) and Pee Dee (for a South Carolina river).

His brother then took out an atlas, looked at Southern rivers, and suggested "Suwannee," which Stephen deliberately misspelled to the two-syllable "Swanee" to fit the melody.

The Stephen Foster Monument in Pittsburgh, Pennsylvania, by sculptor Giuseppe Moretti

Rivers

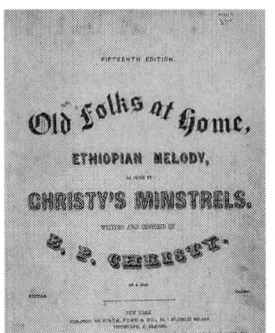

After Stephen Foster wrote the song, he sold it to a businessman, E.P. Christy, who ran a number of minstrel shows and who actually took credit for it on one of the song sheets. (See image to the left.) Christy paid Foster for the credit line, and Foster agreed, something the composer later regretted.

In 1935, a state representative from Miami sponsored a bill to make "Swanee River" Florida's official state song, replacing "Florida, My Florida," which the State Legislature had adopted in 1913.

Here were the original first stanza and chorus the way Foster wrote them:

"Old Folks at Home"

Way down upon de Swanee Ribber,
Far, far away,
Dere's wha my heart is turning ebber,
Dere's wha de old folks stay.
All up and down de whole creation
Sadly I roam,
Still longing for de old plantation,
And for de old folks at home.

CHORUS
All de world am sad and dreary,
Eb-rywhere I roam;
Oh, darkeys, how my heart grows weary,
Far from de old folks at home!

Florida's Official Song

Over time, the original words, which were supposedly in the words of a black slave at a time (1851) when slavery was legal in half the states, became more and more offensive. In 1978, the phrase "still longing for de old plantation" became "still longing for my old connection" in the seventh line of the first stanza, and the word "brothers" was substituted for "darkeys" in the third line of the chorus.

A mural in the Stephen Foster Folk Culture Center State Park in White Springs along the Suwannee depicts a scene from the song.

In 2008, the Florida Legislature decreed that the official version contain the revised lyrics. State officials also sponsored a contest for a new state song. In 2008, they chose "Florida, Where the Sawgrass Meets the Sky" as a replacement, but that song later became the state's official anthem.

The Stephen Foster Folk Culture Center State Park in White Springs

The Suwannee River is spectacular in beauty.

"Old Folks at Home" is still the state song, but the officially reworked lyrics today are less offensive.

One wonders how many people in this country and abroad first came to know Florida through Stephen Foster's wonderful song. I have heard totally unsubstantiated rumors that the composer once secretly made it to North Florida and saw the river that he made famous, but I doubt if he ever did come here. It doesn't matter.

The song will live on, especially in its cleaned-up version, for generations to come.

Chapter 5: The Ghost Town of Columbus

Ghost towns have always interested me. To think that the abandoned place in front of you was once a thriving village/town with lots of residents, all of whom had high hopes for their futures. And then, for some unexpected reason, the people moved away, the railroad bypassed the town, steamboats went elsewhere, or flood/disease/storm made it an undesirable place to live.

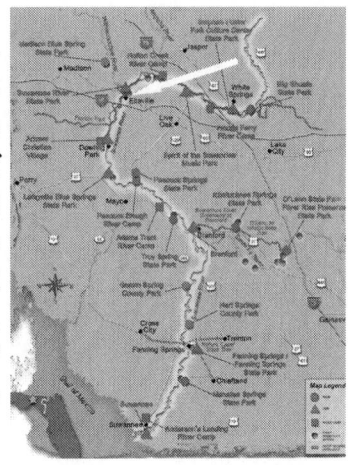

We have many such towns in Florida, especially in the interior of the state. One such town is Columbus, which stood on the Suwannee River in the present-day Suwannee River State Park near Live Oak (see white arrow on the map above).

In the mid-1800s, Columbus had about 500 inhabitants. Its sister city across the Suwannee was Ellaville, where George Drew, the first governor of Florida elected after Reconstruction, had a house and lumber mill.

The location was ideal for commerce since nearby is the junction of the Suwannee and Withlacoochee rivers.

The Suwannee (on the right) joins the Withlacoochee near Columbus.

Steamboats used to be able to go up to Columbus and transport some three thousand bales of cotton in a year. An 1843 newspaper description of the town mentioned a beautiful boiling spring and rich, fertile lands in the vicinity.

During the Civil War Columbus had an earth-works facility from which Confederate soldiers could guard the old railroad bridge from Union attack. A stagecoach stop there and a ferry also provided a means of income to the inhabitants, as did a saw mill.

The Confederate earth-works facility at the site of the town

Columbus also used to be the terminus for a twice-a-month mail service by steamboat from Cedar Key on the Gulf of Mexico. Steamboats connected the little settlement of Columbus to the rest of the world, for example New Orleans and Key West.

The Ghost Town of Columbus

A bridge over the Suwannee near Columbus was important for the transportation of cattle, salt, and sugar from Florida to Confederate troops during the Civil War. The site was so important to the Confederate war effort that Union troops from Jacksonville headed west in February 1864, to destroy that bridge and shorten the war, but Confederate troops met and stopped the Union soldiers at the Battle of Ocean Pond at Olustee in Baker County, the largest Civil War battle in Florida.

A modern bridge at the site of the older bridge over the Suwannee

Remnants of an old saw mill at Columbus

By the 1870s, the town for some reason began to decline in importance as the steamboats stopped calling and settlers found other, more desirable places to raise crops.

Today the site of the old Columbus is within the Suwannee River State Park. Among the few remnants of the town is its cemetery, which is one of the oldest in the state. Standing in that final resting place of several residents of Columbus can give one an eerie feeling of being in the vicinity of where a formerly important town once prospered.

The cemetery at Columbus is one of the few remnants of the ghost town there.

Apalachicola River

Introduction to the river

The Apalachicola River, one of the most threatened rivers in Florida, is about 112 miles (180 km) long in the Panhandle and flows into the Gulf of Mexico. The river, whose head waters are in northeast Georgia, extends 500 miles (800 km) and is fed by the Flint and Chattachoochee rivers (see to the right the map of the two rivers joining the Apalachicola). Its name comes from the Native Americans who lived in the area hundreds of years ago: the Apalachicola Tribe.

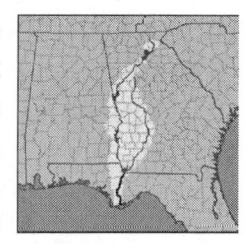

During Florida's British Colonial Period (1763–1783), the river formed the boundary between East Florida and West Florida.

Among the natural beauties along the river are Torreya State Park, Apalachicola National Forest, Apalachicola Bluffs, and Tates Hell State Forest. The basin of the river area also produces tupelo honey, a product that can bring in almost one million dollars a year.

Torreya State Park is part of the river system,

Rivers

Commercial shrimping boats still line the river.

    The river enters the Gulf of Mexico at the small town of Apalachicola, the county seat of Franklin County. With a population of around 2,500, the town relies on tourism, shrimping, and the oyster industry.

    At one point in the 19th century, before the arrival of the railroads, Apalachicola was the third busiest port in the Gulf of Mexico, behind New Orleans and Mobile. The history of the small town includes the development of the cold-air process of refrigeration, the forerunner of air conditioning, by Dr. John Gorrie.

The downtown area is picturesque.

26

Chapter 6: Harvesting Oysters in Apalachicola Bay

Apalachicola Bay in Florida's Panhandle has long been known as one of the most productive areas for harvesting oysters in America. However, since Georgia and Alabama have been diverting the waters from the Apalachicola-Chattahoochee-Flint (ACF) River Basin, waters which eventually make their way into the Apalachicola River, Florida's oystering industry has suffered a very serious blow.

Apalachicola Bay, which includes St. Vincent Sound and St. George Sound, is an ideal area for oysters because the estuary there – with an influx of both sea water and fresh water – has high levels of nutrients, which promote the growth of oysters. The Apalachicola River is an essential part of that estuary, where oysters can reach maturity in only two years.

Scenes like this from the early 1900s may soon be ancient history.

According to oysterguide.com, "Apalachicola is the last place in the United States where wild oysters are still harvested by tongs from small boats." 90% of Florida's oysters come from the bay there.

Oyster shucking in Apalachicola has provided many people with good jobs over the years.

The nutrient-rich Apalachicola Bay allows small oysters to reach market size in about two years, a much shorter time than in the waters further north. Our Florida oysters play a big role in the state's economy, but also in the ecosystem of our waters as they filter and clean the water. Those waters provide habitat for crabs, fish, shrimp, and other sea animals. When it is feeding, a single oyster can filter and clean 25 gallons of water in just 24 hours.

Florida oysters are available during the whole year, but the harvesting of them really is done mostly in the fall as water temperatures fall.

Oyster-gatherers, and that title will often refer to a whole family, in Apalachicola Bay still harvest the oysters from small boats using large, long-handled tongs to scoop them up from the shallow water, a method that has been used for over a hundred years. The fishermen found that dredging, while easier, severely damages oyster beds.

An image from 1909 shows an oyster boat in Apalachicola Bay. A day for those youngsters working such boats would begin at 4 a.m. and last all day long.

Workers have been planting oyster shells in the bay from the early 1900s. In fact, the Florida Department of Agriculture and Consumer Services has collected and planted more than 10 million bushels of shucked oyster shells, a practice which promotes the oyster fishery industry and brings much economic benefit to the oyster-producing counties of Franklin, Levy, and Wakulla.

Rivers

*After young shuckers took the fresh oysters
out of their shells, the youngsters discarded the shells.
This photo from 1909 shows a huge pile of such discarded
shells in Florida. Other workers used
the shells to make railroad beds and streets.*

In 2013, federal officials declared a fishery disaster for Florida's oyster industry in the Gulf of Mexico, a disaster caused by a prolonged drought and the increasing siphoning off of water from the two major rivers flowing into the Apalachicola River, siphoning by Georgia (to satisfy the water needs of thirsty Atlanta) and by Alabama (to support its huge agricultural industry).

What happens to the oyster business in Apalachicola Bay depends in a way less on weather patterns than on politicians from the three affected states (Alabama, Florida, and Georgia) to agree on a fair and promising method of allocating the valuable waters of the river that has provided thousands of people with work for centuries.

Chapter 7: Ferries on North Florida Rivers

Long before engineers built wooden or iron bridges across North Florida rivers, people used basic, wooden contraptions to cross the waterways.

In fact, for many years such ferries provided the only means for crossing the rivers, especially in the deeper parts.

Early entrepreneurs in the 19th century set up ferries for themselves and as a business to take others across the river. When Spain ceded the territory of Florida to the United States in 1821, newly arrived settlers sometimes found ferries already operating on the rivers. Some of those ferries, then, have had a long history.

A Suwannee River ferry transporting a car

Rivers

Ferry operators tried to be politically neutral, which meant that they would transport anyone with the necessary fare. For example, Robert Martin, who operated a ferry on the Suwannee at Wilcox Landing above Fort Fanning, transported both Confederate and Union soldiers during the Civil War. The Confederate Army actually drafted him, but – realizing how important his work was to their cause – allowed him to continue as a ferryman.

Different kinds of ferries on the Suwannee

Between 1901 and 1904, Kate Roberts and her son, J.R. Roberts, operated the ferry across the Suwannee near Wilcox Landing. They carried passengers and also merchandise from Mrs. Roberts's store to settlers in the area. The fares they charged to cross the river were as follows:

>5 cents for a man on foot
>15 cents for a man and horse
>25 cents for a single team
>40 cents for a double buggy
>50 cents for a double wagon

The Rock Bluff Ferry ran for many years between present-day Dixie County and Gilchrist County. Local residents called it the Free Ferry because there was no charge to use it to cross the Suwannee. The two counties paid for its operation.

This ferry would accommodate only one vehicle at a time and was held on its course by a steel cable about one inch (2.5 cm) in diameter, which was securely tied to large oaks on each side of the river. With a wooden tool that slipped over the cable, the operator would pull the ferry across by sliding the tool over the cable. Whenever steamboats would come by, the ferryman would lower the cable deep enough into the water so that it would not interfere with the boats.

Two more Florida ferries from the early 20th century

Rivers

The 74-mile-long (119 km) Ocklawaha River near Ocala in Marion County was a typical Florida river in that farmers and ranchers used it to transport goods, many of those goods by ferry.

The images below from the Library of Congress show what some of those early ferries looked like.

Chapter 8: Boating Parties on North Florida Rivers

For hundreds of years, Floridians and their guests have known the pleasure of spending a day on one of our rivers. The archives around the Southeast, especially in the very accessible Florida State Archives in Tallahassee, have treasure troves of information, biographies, genealogies, and photographs, including some of late 19th-century and early 20th-century people enjoying a day on a river or lake..

The first photo (below), that of a boating party out for a picnic, shows Dunns Creek in the 1880s. Dunns Creek is a waterway about 17 miles (27 km) south of Palatka that joins the St. Johns River to Crescent Lake. (For the story of a famous shipwreck in Dunns Creek, see Chapter 2 in this book.) What may be most notable about the guests on these boats is how well dressed they were. Shorts and cut-offs would not appear in such settings until the late 20th century.

Rivers

The second photo shows The *Okeehumkee* on the Ocklawaha River in 1881. That vessel was the longest-serving steamboat on that river. The boat had a shallow draft, which enabled it to maneuver the narrow, winding river. Its engine and paddle wheel were somewhat hidden in the lower part of the steamboat. It was much larger than the other party boats in this chapter, but no doubt was a favorite among Floridians.

The third photo shows the Tomoka River in 1888. After the St. Johns and Halifax rivers, the Tomoka is the longest river in Volusia County at around 20 miles (32 km).

Boating Parties on North Florida Rivers

The Tomoka River begins in the woods near Daytona Beach at an elevation of 23 feet (7 meters) and flows north – northeast through Daytona Beach and Ormond Beach until it empties into the Halifax River.

Notice in the previous photo the three elegantly dressed women in the photo as they gaze at a small alligator, presumably dead, being held by one man while another, maybe the hunter, watches on.

The fourth photo (below) also shows the Tomoka in 1888. Here a mate pulls the boat to shore while those on board prepare to go onto land.

One lady in the bow is practicing her aim with a gun. Passengers on such boats used to delight in shooting gators and other animals from the safety of the boat.

Rivers

The fifth photo (above) pictures two boats at Tomoka Landing near Ormond in 1898. The man in the smaller boat may be pulling the larger boat away from shore before it could head on its way.

The last photo (to the right) shows a group of people enjoying Silver Springs in the 1880s.

Such photographs give us a brief glimpse into what pleasure our waterways provided our ancestors over a hundred years ago.

II: Lakes in North Florida: Introduction

Florida has thousands of lakes. In fact, Charles Boning points out in his *Florida's Rivers* that we have 7,700 named lakes. (Look in the bibliography at the back of this book for a list of the books cited.) We also know that we get drenched each year to the tune of some 53 inches (135 cm) of rain, making us one of the wettest states in the country, after Hawaii, Louisiana, Mississippi, and Alabama. Although much of that water is lost to evaporation, much of it also falls into our rivers and lakes and streams.

We have a whole county, Lake, so named because of the approximately 1,400 named lakes within its boundaries. The many lakes make up almost 18% of the county's area. If you ever fly in a plane to/from Orlando over the county, you will be amazed at the many lakes there.

The navigable channel for boats entering Lake George from the south on the St. Johns River in Volusia County

Lakes

Lake George, pictured on the previous page, is the second largest lake in the state, after Lake Okeechobee.

Floridians may not realize that Lake George was named by royal botanist John Bartram, the father of famed explorer William Bartram, for England's King George III at a time (1763–1783) when this territory belonged to Great Britain.

Lake Okeechobee is the seventh largest freshwater lake in the country and the second largest that is contained completely within the lower 48 states; Lake Michigan is the largest. Okeechobee is, however, the largest freshwater lake that is completely within a single state of the lower 48.

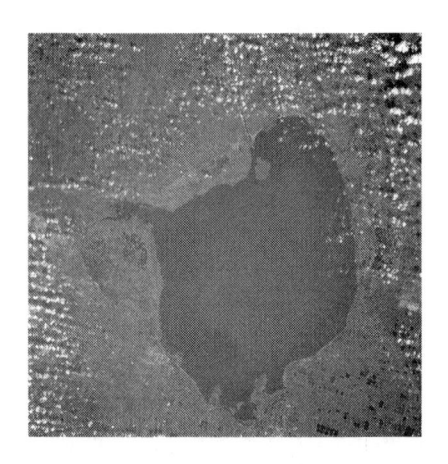

Lake Okeechobee as seen from space

We will look at two lakes in North Florida: Newnans Lake and Lake Harris.

Chapter 9: Indian Canoes in Newnans Lake

Florida lakes are known for good fishing, gator and bird watching, sailing, and – in an amazing stroke of luck – preserving canoes in various stages of construction from hundreds of years ago. That find was made possible by a severe drought that affected much of Florida in the early 2000s. In that decade, the lack of rain caused rivers and lakes to recede and sometimes disappear. It also revealed what was on the bottom of lakes, much to the delight of archaeologists.

Because lakes do not normally have the water movement that rivers have, they merit special attention from volunteer monitors, ordinary citizens who keep tabs on the condition of local lakes. In 1991, the Florida Legislature, recognizing the importance of such a program, established in our statutes Florida LAKEWATCH, one of the largest lake-monitoring programs in the country.

Native Americans, including Seminoles (shown here making a canoe in the Everglades), have been using canoes on the rivers and lakes of this state for hundreds, maybe several thousand years.

Lakes

*A Seminole Indian and family in a dug-out canoe
near Miami in the early 20th century*

One particular lake, Newnans Lake near Gainesville, which is normally known for good sailing and fishing (black crappie, bluegill, largemouth bass, shellcracker, and sunshine bass), was hiding something of far more interest to archaeologists.

In 2000, students from Gainesville's Eastside High School, led by their environmental-science teacher, examined the exposed north shore of nearby Newnans Lake and discovered 101 canoes, some only partially finished. The mud from the 5,800-acre lake had preserved the canoes for hundreds of years.

Most of the canoes were made out of Southern hard pine, while others were made of cypress and conifers. Radiocarbon dating indicated that the canoes were between 500 and 5,000 years old. The canoes varied in size from 15 to 31 feet (4.6 - 9.5 meters) in length.

The find was the largest of its kind ever and helped scientists know much about ancient watercraft and how the earliest residents of the peninsula navigated on Florida waterways. While state officials moved some of the fragile vessels to preservation tanks in Tallahassee, they allowed the rest to be inundated once again by the rising lake waters.

Extracting a centuries-old canoe from muck, which has preserved the canoe from deterioration, is time-consuming and arduous.

Early European and American travelers sometimes mentioned such canoes. For example, in 1774 naturalist William Bartram visited the Suwannee River and wrote the following about the Seminoles he saw: "These Indians have large handsome canoes [carved] out of the trunks of Cypress trees, some of them commodious enough to accommodate 20 or 30 warriors. In these . . . they descend the river on trading and hunting expeditions on the sea coast, neighboring islands and keys . . . and sometimes cross the gulph [of Mexico], extending their navigations to the Bahama Islands and even to Cuba."

Newnans Lake was named for Daniel Newnan, a Georgia militia officer who fought the Seminoles near the lake in 1812. The Seminole name for the lake was *Pithlachocco*, meaning "place of the long boats," which may have indicated that the lake was the site of a canoe-making operation.

Lakes

Those who find Indian canoes should not remove them, but instead notify local authorities. The state owns lake beds, even those that are dried out, and also canoes extracted from protective mud can quickly deteriorate when the air hits them.

Canoes have been found throughout Florida, for example at DeLeon Springs in Volusia County and on a peat farm in Clay County.

Preserving such finds and displaying them in museums will make them available for countless visitors for decades to come.

For many people, for example historians and archaeologists, finding such rare Indian canoes is discovering a great treasure that can reveal the lifestyle and habits of our predecessors dating back several thousand years.

An illustration of North Florida Indians in a canoe from the 16th century

Chapter 10: Lake Harris

Typical of the many beautiful lakes in North Florida is Lake Harris, the largest body of water in Lake County, Florida. It is about 30 miles (48 km) northwest of Orlando and receives most of its water from the Palatlakaha River, a name which meant "swamp-big-site" in an Indian language.

The name of the lake honors an earlier pioneer in the region, Ebenezer Harris (1815–1885), who lived at Yalaha in the 1840s; or it honors a Colonel Frank Harris, who lived near the lake with his family during the Seminole Indian Wars of the 19th century.

The Seminole name for the lake was *Astatulq*, which according to *Florida Place Names* by Allen Morris meant "lake of sunbeams, lake of sparkling moonbeams, people of different tribes, or arrow."

Lake Harris is popular with boaters and fishermen.

Lakes

One of the major social activities of Lake Harris residents in the 19th century was the bear hunt, which was organized by a bear club. The bears in the area were so abundant that they would steal pigs from the barns and under the houses of the people there. At one of the weekly hunts, one of the hunters killed a 400-pound (181-kg) bear. Other animals in the vicinity were alligators (which preyed on horses and cattle), panthers, red wolves, and wild turkeys (which would eat the crops).

Lake Harris has much open space around it.

Lake Harris is part of eight interconnected bodies of water called the Harris Chain, which cover about fifty thousand acres of water. The lakes average 10-12 feet (3-3.7 m) in depth, with Big Lake Harris the deepest at 30 feet (9.1 m) along the southern shoreline. The lakes are connected by canals, which allow boaters to go from one to another.

Lake Harris

Relatively few homes are on the lake.

Lake Harris and its interconnected lakes used to be much better for bass fishing and hosted at least one major tournament, but the spraying of weeds, as well as locks, pollution from Lake Apopka, and some mysterious bass viruses greatly hurt the fishing.

The over-use of herbicides and the introduction of grass carp to the lakes in the 1980s caused major problems. When hydrilla became prevalent in the lakes, officials had workers use new chemicals to eradicate the invasive plant.

Workers managed to kill off the hydrilla in the late 1980s, but – in doing so – they also severely damaged native-plant species. Pepper and eel grass became lifeless muck which sank to the bottom of the lakes. The loss of cover drove the bass away, and bass tournaments fared badly for several decades.

Lakes

By 2013, Lake Harris and the other nearby lakes were in much better shape. The grass carp were long gone, and bass fishing markedly improved. Much of the credit goes to those water officials who decided to let the lakes determine their own levels rather than keep the water levels artificially high. The result has been that the shorelines are cleaner than before. Officials also try to manage hydrilla rather than trying to eliminate it completely.

Other reasons for the return of Lake Harris to productive fishing grounds are the daily limit of bass for fishermen; catch-and-release programs; the replanting of reeds; and building a water-filtering facility to clean the water from Lake Apopka. Fishermen have high hopes that Lake Harris and the other bodies of water will return to formerly very productive fishing grounds.

Lake Harris has considerably improved from the past.

III: Springs in North Florida: Introduction

One of the greatest natural assets of Florida's waterways, especially in North Florida, is the spring. According to Doug Stamm in his *Springs of Florida*, the state has more than 300 springs. We may actually have twice that number, although some are very small. At least 21 known springs are in Florida's state parks. The springs have been attracting people to the peninsula for thousands of years.

A 2004 report entitled *Florida Geological Survey Bulletin 66* named over 700 springs, 33 of which were first magnitude, 191 were second magnitude, and 151 were third magnitude. A first-magnitude spring has an average flow of more than 100 cubic feet per second, which equals 64.6 million gallons per day. A second-magnitude spring has an average flow between 10 and 100 cubic feet per second. A third-magnitude spring has an average flow of less than 10 cubic feet per second or 6.46 million gallons a day.

Manatee Springs off the Suwannee River

Springs

The water outflow of many springs in Florida has diminished sharply in the last twenty years because of a severe drought and increased pumping of water from the Florida Aquifer. Some springs have completely dried up, for example White Springs and Worthington Springs.

Today more than a dozen Florida cities have "Spring" in their name. Among the most popular name for springs is "Blue," so much so that the county name was added to "Blue Spring," for example Volusia Blue Spring.

Among the most prominent organizations devoted to the preservation of our springs is The Howard T. Odum Florida Springs Insitute, founded by Dr. Robert Knight and named for Dr. Howard Odum (1924–2002), an American ecologist. For more about the Springs Institute see its web site: http://floridaspringsinstitute.org/.

Gornto (Guaranto) Springs in Dixie County

Here I consider two representative springs in North Florida.

Chapter 11: Hart Springs

Hart Springs is part of a park in Gilchrist County billed as "one of the largest spring-fed swimming areas in the state of Florida." The facilities there are suitable for birding, camping, fishing, hiking, picnicking, and swimming.

The park is one of the designated camps on the Suwannee River Wilderness Trail, a system of public and private recreation and visitor facilities along the river. Divers and swimmers should consult the following web site for more information about Hart Springs: www.hartsprings.com/diving.html.

The park at Hart Springs has many parts and caters to many different kinds of interests.

Springs

In the early 2000s, cave diving was illegal at Hart Springs because the cave was clogged. Workers had brought in sand, some of it from the main spring vent, and spread it around the edge of the basin to make a comfortable beach for swimmers and sunbathers.

The sand had ended up at the main vent when the spring had reversed flow during the flooding of the river. That sand and other sand that fell into the vent from the motion of swimmers blocked the flow considerably.

Cave divers, as they have often done throughout Florida, worked on clearing the vent of debris and sand with the help of a hydraulic dredge-pump from the Suwannee River Water Management District. They also used lift bags to extract tons of rock and concrete from the spring head.

The park at Hart Springs connects to the Suwannee.

Hart Springs

The long boardwalk leads from the park to the river.

As at other state parks along Florida rivers, Hart Springs features a very long boardwalk that allows visitors to walk through different kinds of Florida landscape and not get their feet wet. The boardwalk wanders through the park and along the river, giving a good view of the Suwannee.

It also allows the visitor to see different kinds of docks, for example floating docks that can rise and fall with fluctuations in the depth of the water (see image to the left).

Springs

Hart Springs and other such sites along the Suwannee are subject to flooding. The Suwannee River Water Management District, which monitors the river, notes on its web site (http://www.srwmd.state.fl.us/index.aspx) that a flood stage "is the water level at which some type of physical or economic hardship occurs along a river. It does not necessarily mean that water is over the banks of the river."

The National Weather Service determines the flood stages based on input from the community and local emergency managers.

A notice on a pole at Hart Springs indicates what year flooding took place there and how high above the mean sea level the water reached.

Those who live along the Suwannee know by now that they need to be aware of what is happening in and around the upper stages of the river. For example, if it rains heavily in the Okefenokee Swamp, a shallow waterland that straddles the Florida – Georgia border, much of that water will eventually make its way to the Suwannee. Because the Okefenokee is relatively shallow, but large (438,000 acres, 1,770 km^2), the water does not permeate into the earth as it does in other large swamps.

Residents along the river who have experienced flooded homes and inaccessibility to their property know that they must pay attention to the weather north of them, i.e. in North Florida and South Georgia.

Chapter 12: Wakulla Springs

One of the most famous cinematic sites in Florida is Wakulla Springs, which is about 14 miles (23 km) south of Tallahassee and 5 miles (8 km) east of Crawfordville. It is part of the Edward Ball Wakulla Springs State Park. Ed Ball (1888 – 1981) was a powerful businessman, the brother-in-law of industrialist Alfred duPont, and the developer of the St. Joe Company, which owned much land in Florida's Panhandle.

One of the glass-bottomed boats at Wakulla Springs

Wakulla Springs, the longest and one of the deepest submerged cave systems in the whole world, is a first-magnitude spring, meaning that it has an average flow of more than 100 cubic feet per second, which equals 64.6 million gallons per day. The springs flow into Wakulla River, which flows for nine miles (14 km) before joining the St. Marks River, which flows into the Gulf of Mexico.

The earliest human residents of the area were what are called Paleo-Indians, who lived near the springs more than 12,000 years ago. They were descended from those people who crossed over the Bering Strait from Asia during the Pleistocene Epoch, which spanned the time period from over 2 million years ago to 11,700 years ago.

Springs

In the mid-19th century archaeologists discovered in Wakulla Springs the remains of some ten extinct mammals, which go back to the last glacial period or Ice Age, which lasted from 110,000 to 10,000 years ago. Scientists found the fossils hundreds of feet back in a cave in the springs.

Also, because water levels used to be much lower than they are today, divers have found the charcoal remnants of fires, which show that Ice-Age peoples lived there at a time when the caves were dry.

Divers looking for fossils deep in Wakulla Springs

Among the fossils retrieved from the caves in the springs were those of a mastodon, an extinct species related to elephants. The mastodons lived in herds in forests and no doubt frequented the clear springs for the fresh water.

The bones of the mastodon recovered in Wakulla Springs are now on display at the Museum of Florida History, which is in the Grey Building in Tallahassee.

Wakulla Springs

A mastodon like this creature probably once roamed Florida near Wakulla Springs.

In the 1950s and 1960s, divers from Florida State University found human tools made from bone and stone, which could indicate that early humans lived near the springs.

Among the animals found today at Wakulla Springs (and certainly at other Florida springs) are otters, snapping turtles, softshell turtles, Suwannee River cooters, West Indian manatees, white-tailed deer, many kinds of birds (anhingas, bald eagles, black vultures, common moorhens, ducks, egrets, herons, limpkins, ospreys, purple gallinules, turkey vultures), and of course alligators.

Occasionally, there are reports at the springs of a gator attack on an unsuspecting swimmer, but in those rare instances the swimmer has swum far beyond the restricted area where it is safe to swim.

One can see families of deer at Wakulla Springs.

Springs

The clarity and quality of the water at Wakulla Springs led to the filming of several movies there, including early Tarzan films that starred Johnny Weissmuller, e.g. "Tarzan's New York Adventure."

Other films shot there were "Creature from the Black Lagoon" (1954), "Night Moves" (1975), "Joe Panther" (1976), and "Airport '77" (1977).

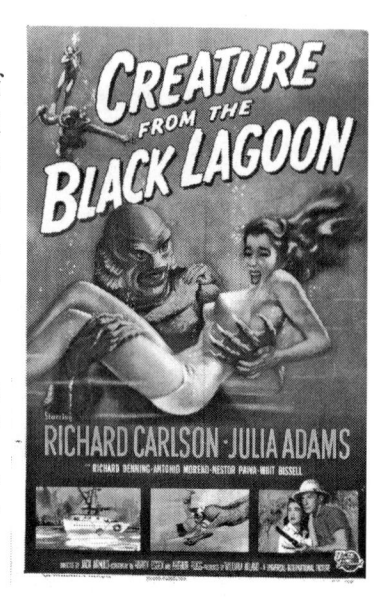

Today, the park has guided riverboat tours and – when the water is clear – glass-bottom boats. It also offers swimming, a nature trail, a lodge, and a dining room.

Officials placed the park on the National Register of Historic Places and named it a National Natural Landmark. The park is especially popular in the hot summer months. As always, divers need to be careful when going into the underwater caves. They should never dive alone.

A diving platform at the park today

IV: Shipwrecks in North Florida: Introduction

With a coastline of about 1,350 miles (2,170 km), Florida ranks behind only Alaska – with its 33,904 miles (54,563 km). And that does not count the miles of land bordering rivers and lakes and other bodies of water.

Because the Florida peninsula sticks out toward the Caribbean and Atlantic Ocean, it has been subject to storms, including hurricanes, for thousands of years. Those storms, battles, and human error have caused many ships to sink. In fact, historians and archaeologists have documented over 2,000 shipwrecks along our coast. No one knows how many other countless vessels still lie beneath our offshore waters.

Detonations aboard the decommissioned USS Oriskany *sent it to the bottom of the sea off Pensacola to become an artificial reef in 2006. After 25 years of service in the U.S. Navy, the ship would help the marine life, fishing, and diving off the Florida Panhandle.*

Such shipwrecks have allowed many divers to explore them, photograph them, and report on the countless fish that make their home in the wrecks. Some ships, deemed to be past their useful above-water life, have been deliberately sunk to make artificial reefs.

The USS destroyer Basilone, *pictured here in the late 1960s or early 1970s, served in the U.S. Navy after World War II. She was decommissioned in 1977 and sunk in 1982 in the Atlantic Ocean off St. Augustine to become an artificial reef.*

These shipwrecks are part of underwater archaeological preserves that the State of Florida has established to preserve the wrecks and to encourage divers to explore the ships rather than coral reefs. The sites have an explanatory underwater plaque; a brochure and laminated underwater guides are available from local dive shops.

The parks are open to the public year round, free of charge. For a virtual experience on these sites and more information on the preserves see this site: www.museumsinthesea.com. The next chapters examine several Florida shipwrecks in North Florida: one in the St. Johns River, one in the Suwannee River, and one in the Atlantic Ocean off Daytona Beach.

Chapter 13: *Maple Leaf*

The artifacts found in shipwrecks, whether in Florida waters or elsewhere, are not always gold and silver. In fact, to the historian and archaeologist, a ship encased in mud or sand is a time capsule that can preserve for decades and even centuries the artifacts and everyday utensils from a distant past.

This is the case with the finding of a Civil War transport steamer, the *Maple Leaf*, in the St. Johns River in the 1980s. The shaving kits, clothing, daguerreotypes, and personal belongings of the Union soldiers on board the vessel can educate new generations about life during the American Civil War.

An illustration of the Maple Leaf *right before it hit a torpedo and sank in the St. Johns River in 1864*

Shipwrecks

The ship was built in 1851 in Kingston, Ontario, as a luxury passenger and freight vessel. The 181-foot (55-meter) side-wheel steamer had three decks. When the Civil War began, American businessmen bought her for a troop transport, and then, in 1862, federal officials chartered the ship for transporting army troops.

In the spring of 1864, Union troops loaded the ship with 400 tons of baggage near Charleston, South Carolina, for a trip to Jacksonville, Florida, where the soldiers were going to reinforce their comrades against an expected Confederate attack. Confederate troops had defeated Union troops at the Battle of Olustee in February 1864, west of Jacksonville, and might have been planning to recapture the city.

When the *Maple Leaf* arrived in Jacksonville in March 1864, local authorities ordered her to transport some 90 cavalrymen and their horses 60 miles (97 km) south to Palatka. She was to proceed immediately, even before the troops could unload the cargo from South Carolina. In Palatka, the ship unloaded the cavalrymen and their horses, picked up three Confederate prisoners and a small group of Union sympathizers who were fleeing the area, and headed north back to Jacksonville.

This kind of "torpedo" (now called a mine) sank the ship.

Maple Leaf

When the ship was near Mandarin Point twelve miles (19 km) south of Jacksonville, it hit a beer-keg mine with about 70 pounds of explosive powder and exploded. Four deck hands who were sleeping on the ship's bow died, but the other passengers survived. The ship sank within seven minutes in 24 feet (7.3 meters) of water, but part of the structure remained above water. The survivors piled into lifeboats and headed for Jacksonville.

Confederate troops later arrived on the scene and set the remains of the ship on fire, but decided not to try to retrieve the cargo. As time passed, the ship slowly sank into the bottom of the river until about seven feet (2 m) of mud covered the wreck. And there it remained for 121 years.

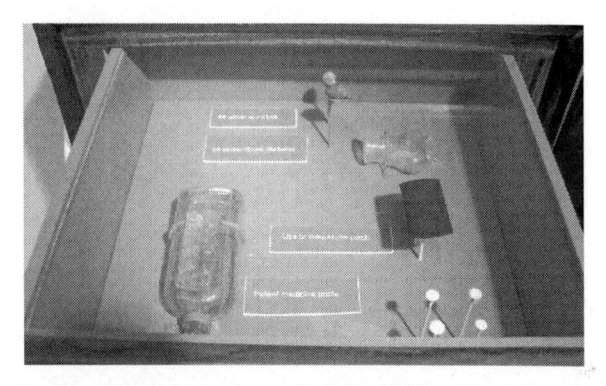

A display of artifacts from the Maple Leaf *in a local museum*

The mud and lack of oxygen effectively preserved the remains of the ship during the ensuing years. In the 1980s, a Jacksonville dentist, Keith Holland, the great-great-grandson of an Alabama Confederate soldier, began researching records in libraries, the National Archives, and the Department of Justice before he was able to pinpoint the site of the wreck.

Divers discovered the wreck in 1984, but did not positively identify it until 1992. Two years later, officials declared the site a National Historic Landmark.

Divers have recovered over a thousand pounds (454 kg) of the ship's cargo, but the work is difficult because they have to work in poor visibility conditions caused by the tannic acid of the river. As with other sites, the divers need official permits to allow them to dive on and excavate such a site.

The divers have displayed many of the artifacts in local Jacksonville museums. Those artifacts have given historians a good perspective on what soldiers of the Civil War carried with them, for example everyday items like sewing utensils and repair kits for fixing worn-out items like shoes and clothing.

The ship is telling us much about the ordinary life of the foot soldier and therefore adding knowledge about our military past.

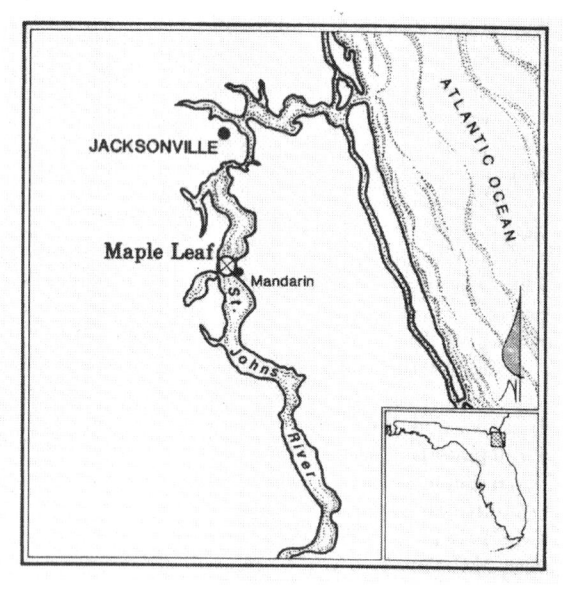

The wreck is near Mandarin, Florida, on the St. Johns.

Chapater 14: *City of Hawkinsville*

Before railroads began to inch their way down and across Florida in the 19th century, merchants and travelers relied on steamboats to reach the more inaccessible parts of the peninsula, especially those on inland waterways. The fact that the Suwannee and Apalachicola rivers ran north-south enabled steamboats to cover much of the state and encouraged new arrivals to settle on those rivers.

Beginning in 1834, steamboats began navigating the Suwannee, at first sticking to the lower river below Branford, but later venturing as far north as Columbus, now a ghost town in Suwannee River State Park, as discussed above.

An illustration of the City of Hawkinsville

During the American Civil War, traffic on such rivers as the Suwannee was curtailed because of the danger of attack by each side. Steamboat traffic resumed after the war, as enterprising pilots navigated their boats up from Cedar Key, full of groceries, hardware, and clothing for the many residents along the river. They would then make the return trip carrying cotton and produce for sale in Cedar Key and elsewhere.

The steamboat traffic to and from Cedar Key diminished dramatically after 1896, when a hurricane that year severely damaged the little town. Among the few steamboats to continue plying the river was the *City of Hawkinsville*, a 319-ton sternwheeler that served Cedar Key, Old Town, Clays Landing, and Branford.

The City of Hawkinsville *near Thomas Yearty's mill at Vista on the Suwannee River*

Built in Abbeville, Georgia, in 1896, the ship stretched 141 feet (43 meters) and had two decks, a single stack, a square stern, and a molded bow. She was supposed to have served for several years in Georgia waters for the Hawkinsville Deepwater Boat Lines carrying naval stores, but in 1900 the Gulf Transportation Company bought her to transport cedar for pencil factories at Cedar Key, as well as lumber and other goods to and from towns along the Suwannee.

City of Hawkinsville

The City of Hawkinsville of Tampa *at Branford on the Suwannee*

Her official name became *City of Hawkinsville of Tampa* because she was registered at the Port of Tampa. One of her jobs may have been to help in the building of the rail bridge at Old Town, a task that hastened her own obsolescence when the railroads arrived.

She served on the river until 1922, at which time steamboating on the Suwannee ended because of such factors as the coming of the railroad and roads to carry trucks. The owners of the proud vessel apparently abandoned her in the river near the trestle bridge that used to carry the railroad over the river. Workers removed the top deck of the steamboat because it presented an above-water traffic hazard.

Bronson High School principal Michael McCaskill, who discovered the shipwreck when he was a teenager growing up in the area, used to take students from Bronson's Marine Science course to the site to learn more about it.

Another steamboat on the Suwannee was called Three States.

Shipwrecks

The fresh water of the river has helped preserve the wood and metal parts of the vessel, but river currents and occasional fluctuations in the river's depth have eroded exposed timbers. The Suwannee there is often clear enough for divers to have a good view of the ship's main deck, hull, and mechanical equipment, although the visibility below the surface can be poor because of the river's tannic acid color, caused by decaying plant life and the cypress trees along the banks.

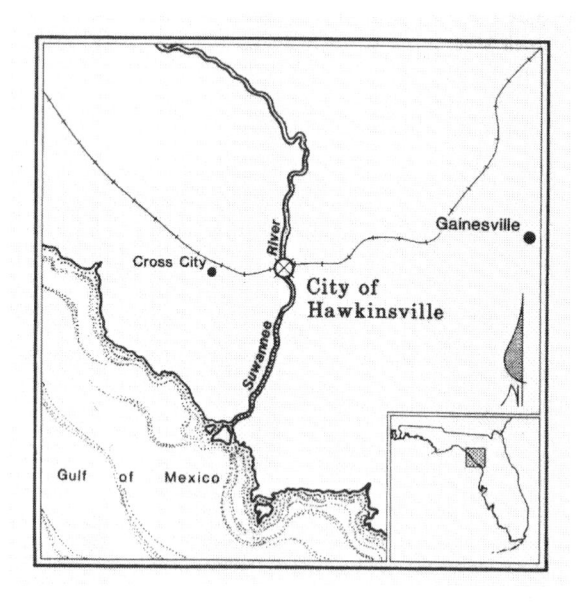

A map showing the location of the shipwreck

In 1991, the Florida Department of State dedicated the site near Old Town on the Dixie side of the Suwannee as an underwater shipwreck park to instruct visitors about steamboating on the river. That particular shipwreck offers a glimpse into a hard-working steamboat that served towns along the river for several decades.

Chapter 15: *Commodore*

Among the 2,000+ documented shipwrecks that have occurred in and off Florida, one led to a short story that ranks as among the best in American Literature. It involved a near-death experience for a renowned journalist/fiction writer off the coast of Daytona Beach. The result was a short story that allows readers, even to this day, to vicariously experience a shipwreck and 30 hours on an angry sea in a little dinghy.

The writer was Stephen Crane, 25-year-old author of *The Red Badge of Courage* (1895), who signed on to go to Cuba to write newspaper articles about Cuba's struggle for independence from Spain. To get to Cuba, he signed on a vessel, *Commodore*, as an able seaman for $20 a month.

An illustration of the Commodore

Shipwrecks

The 178-ton steamship, *Commodore*, built in Philadelphia in 1882 and based out of New York, was 123 feet (37 meters) long and 21 feet (6.4 m) wide. It had a single, coal-fired engine. When the ship left Jacksonville for Cuba on December 31, 1896, she carried a cache of arms for those insurgents fighting for independence from Spain. Because America would not be officially at war with Spain for another 16 months, gunrunning was illegal, but that did not stop arms merchants.

Pictures of Stephen Crane

Soon after the ship left the Jacksonville harbor on her way to Mayport and the open sea, she struck a sandbar at Commodore's Point in the St. Johns River and had to wait until a revenue cutter could tow her off. The captain of the *Commodore* failed to have divers check for damage to the hull, which had probably been weakened from the grounding.

Later at sea, the heavy pounding from the waves weakened her further and she sprang a leak. When the engine room flooded, the pumps could not keep up with the inrushing water. About 18 miles (29 km) off Mosquito Inlet (now Ponce de Leon Inlet) south of Daytona Beach, the captain ordered all hands to abandon ship.

While others panicked, Crane kept his calm demeanor and was the first to volunteer in any way the captain could use him. Before getting into the dinghy, Crane stood on the bridge scanning the horizon with binoculars, trying to figure out the best direction to go.

While the crew went into different lifeboats, Crane and three others scampered into a ten-foot (3-m) dinghy just before the *Commodore* sank and headed for shore. Because of factors like a strong wind, high waves, even a nearby shark, it took the four desperate men 30 hours to reach shore.

The Ponce de Leon Lighthouse (pictured to the right) was a constant beacon to the men, but it seemed too far to reach easily.

One of the four men drowned after the dinghy overturned close to shore, but the other three made it to safety on the beach. First reports from the scene indicated that Crane had drowned, but later headlines announced "Stephen Crane Safe."

Crane made it back to Jacksonville, where he spent the next few months writing his story about the shipwreck, a story entitled "The Open Boat," one of this country's well-known short stories.

The cold that Crane contracted in that harrowing ordeal on the sea may have weakened him and led to his death from tuberculosis three years later.

Shipwrecks

In 1986, an English professor at Jacksonville University enlisted the help of a veteran diver from Ormond Beach to locate the site of the shipwreck. With careful research and many dives, they located the site and recovered artifacts from the ship.

The depth of the wreck, between 70 and 80 feet (21 - 24 meters), allows divers only 30 minutes of bottom time before they have to replenish their air supply and spend two hours decompressing aboard the dive boat. The water is often murky, with strong currents, and sharks are a constant danger.

In the end, Cuba won her independence from Spain, Stephen Crane wrote a classic American short story, and Florida gained a shipwreck that may provide more information about gunrunning a hundred years ago.

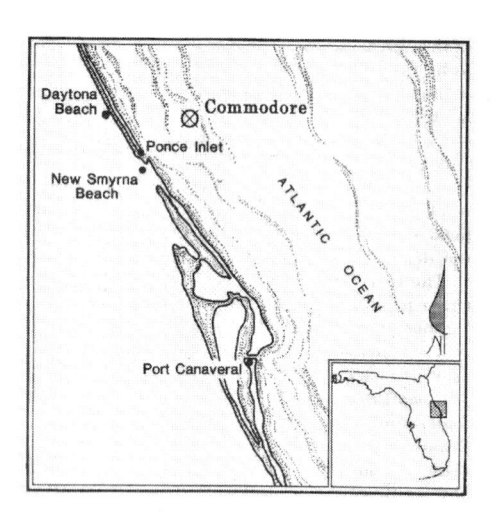

A map showing the location of the shipwreck

V: Watery Critters

This part of the book deals with the many species of what I call "Watery Critters," those fish, reptiles, birds, and animals that live in, on, or under our Florida waters.

This chapter deals with birds that fish in our waters, loggerhead turtles, ugly North Florida fish, and some of the many fish species in our waters.

One might expect to read more about alligators in this section since that reptile is found in many (most?) large bodies of water throughout the state. In fact, it is probably the longest-lasting such animal in all of Florida, dating back thousands of years. I spent my career teaching at the University of Florida, whose mascot is the gator and whose stadium is nicknamed "The Swamp."

I will spend more time in future columns of mine in *Coastal Angler Magazine* and in a second volume of such stories, if there ever is one, dealing with the ever-fascinating gator. But I wanted to concentrate on the birds and fish that boaters and anglers will encounter more often in their forays into our magnficent waterways.

Here is a photo of me holding a live gator (with its mouth taped securely) in the Everglades in 2003.

Watery Critters

Our state has struggled for a long time with invasive species of fish and reptiles (think of pythons in the Everglades), often thrown into our waterways by unsuspecting owners of exotic fish and reptiles who grew tired of how quickly the creatures grew and how much they ate.

In the late 1800s and early 1900s, poachers in Florida killed millions of egrets, flamingos, roseate spoonbills, and other species for their beautiful feathers so that Victorian-era women could flaunt large hats decorated with exotic plumes.

The Everglades in South Florida became a favorite hunting ground for the poachers, who almost wiped out whole species of the colorful birds. Historians estimate that, for several years before 1900, hunters killed more than five million birds every year, including 95 percent of the state's shore birds.

Beautiful birds like these Great Egrets would often be shot on their nests.

We have come a long way in our efforts to protect our wildlife, although – of course – much still needs to be done. Fortunately, most hunters and fishermen seem to be concerned about preserving the environment and protecting species of birds and fish, if for no other reason than to ensure that our descendants will have these beautiful creatures around. The catch-and-release program in our waters has no doubt done much good in making sure that our children and their children have many good-sized fish to catch.

Chapter 16: Birds That Also Fish in North Florida

As any Florida fisherman knows, we're not the only ones who have discovered the pleasures of fishing in our lakes and rivers and creeks. Here are a few other Florida fishers that one can see at any time in North Florida and indeed throughout the state.

The Cormorant pictured here has caught an alligator gar for what will be a large meal if it can digest it. The name of the Cormorant goes back to Latin and means "sea raven." These long-necked diving birds have webbed feet both for underwater propulsion and perching on branches.

The Tri-colored Heron (pictured on the next page) likes to move swiftly in shallow water in pursuit of small fish and sometimes even a small frog or crustacean. The colorful fisher with its slender neck and long bill has a white belly that distinguishes it from other birds, for example the Green Heron. The Tri-coloreds were not as adversely affected by the millinery trade as were the White Egrets, although their numbers have declined in Florida, perhaps from wetland loss.

Watery Critters

The Tri-colored Heron

One of the smartest birds in my opinion is the Green Heron since it uses a kind of tool. It will put an object like a leaf or feather or piece of bread on top of the water. When a curious fish moves in to investigate, the heron will snatch it up for an easy meal.

Its small stocky frame on short legs and a thick neck makes it very distinctive. Note: they are known to poop when flushed out and sent flying.

The Green Heron

Birds That Also Fish in North Florida

And, of course, there is the Brown Pelican, which seems to be ever-present around fish-cleaning stations, looking for a free handout. They also catch fish by plunging into the waters all around the state. One can sometimes see hundreds of them on low, vegetated islands and mangroves.

The Brown Pelican

The Florida bird that probably suffered the most from poachers working in the millinery trade is the Great Egret, pictured here eating a garfish.

The bird's numbers were greatly depleted in the early 20th century by hunters, but laws have put an end to that slaughter, and the birds are making a nice comeback.

And lastly, who can ever forget the sight of an eagle in flight just after he has impaled an unsuspecting fish over a lake? Chances are the majestic bird is taking the fish back to its nest to feed its young'uns.

Eagles will build stick nests, usually high in a tree near water, and add to the structure each year.

The numbers of these birds were reduced in the 1960s because of pesticides in the food chain, but strong conservation methods have saved many species.

Unlike other predators, these wonderful fishers sharing our Florida waterways eat what they catch and don't waste anything. And they sure are pretty to watch.

Chapter 17: Loggerhead Turtles

Usually in May of each year, people around the world celebrate World Turtle Day. That might be a good time to honor turtles, learn more about them, and maybe even stop our car to save one of them on a highway.

Florida boaters and fishermen will likely encounter lots of turtles on our rivers and lakes, so I need to say a few words about the state's official salt water reptile: the Loggerhead Sea Turtle (pictured below).

Florida is one of the two largest nesting areas in the world for that turtle. The other place, Oman in the Middle East, attracts 30,000 females, while Florida's Atlantic Coast has about 25,000. The Florida area is between Cape Canaveral and Sebastian Inlet.

Watery Critters

The lumbering creatures seem to really like the Archie Carr National Wildlife Refuge, named after the University of Florida herpetologist who devoted his career to studying and helping turtles.

The refuge is along Florida's east coast between Melbourne Beach and Wabasso Beach.

A Loggerhead from the underside

Loggerheads begin life on one of our beaches above the high-tide line. After an incubation period of about 80 days, they will come out at night for the first time, when sand temperatures are bearable and when they have more of a chance of escaping capture by a bird or other predator.

A Loggerhead and its reflection in an aquarium

Loggerheads, which have been around for 200 million years, are the most common sea turtle in our state. They can reach a massive size of almost 300 pounds (136 kilograms) and be three feet (almost one meter) long. They can live to the ripe old age of 30, but they also face perils in the sea.

The International Union for the Conservation of Nature considers Loggerheads to be an endangered species. The turtles sometimes die when caught in untended fishing gear or fishing trawls. Concerned fishermen now use turtle excluder devices (TEDs), which allow caught turtles to escape (see image to the right of a sea turtle escaping from a net through a TED).

On land, careless people cause much damage to turtle nests, as do raccoons, which can sometimes devour an entire clutch of turtle eggs. Some local residents protect nesting sites from raccoons by covering the nests with wire mesh.

Signs like this help protect the nesting turtles.

Watery Critters

Another predator that preys on Loggerheads in some areas is the fox.

Like most people, I really like turtles. I have on the outside back wall of my house a three-foot (1-m) by four-foot (1.2-m) mosaic of a giant turtle carrying a holy man across a body of water. I also have a small box turtle that has found a home in my backyard, much to the annoyance of my two dogs.

If my fishermen friends hook one by mistake, they'll gently release it into the water, free to go about foraging for food and avoiding gators. Many volunteers work our beaches during turtle-hatching time to allow the baby turtles to reach the ocean.

So each May, on World Turtle Day, we should probably refrain from having turtle soup, but we should lift a cold drink in honor of a fascinating creature.

Chapter 18: Ugly North Florida Fish

While fishing in Alaska in 2013, I caught what my guide and fishing buddies called "the ugliest fish ever": the Red Irish Lord. Although taking a little umbrage at the disparagement of some of my ancestors, who did in fact build the Blarney Castle in Ireland, I had to agree with their assessment of the fish's lack of good looks. When you look at the attached photo of me holding my ugly fish, you might agree.

And that got me to thinking about the Pantheon of Ugly Florida Fish. I know that beauty is in the eye of the beholder, of course, but maybe some of the readers of this collection of essays will agree with me. Here is my list of really ugly North Florida fish.

The Flathead Catfish (see image to the left), an invasive species that is found in many if not all of the Florida Panhandle rivers, has a mottled brown coloring, wide-set eyes, and large mouth which can really gross out those who have never seen one before. The invasive species has managed to destroy many native fish in this state and for that reason alone ought to be caught till they disappear from our rivers.

Watery Critters

The Lizardfish (see image to the right) are small fish living in tropical and subtropical waters. They take their name from a resemblance to lizards. They also have many sharp teeth, including on their tongue.

The Stargazer, for example the kind found in our waters, has eyes on the top of its head – thus its name. The upward-facing mouth in its large head is also strange, but it uses that mouth to leap up from the sand, in which it is hiding, to devour unsuspecting, passing fish. It will also wiggle a worm-shaped protuberance from its mouth to attract tasty morsels. Its two large poison spines complete the looks of this "ugly" fish. Pictured here is a species called the Common Stargazer.

We should also probably include the Fangtooth Fish, so called because of its large teeth that resemble fangs. And that face will never win any beauty contests in the sea.

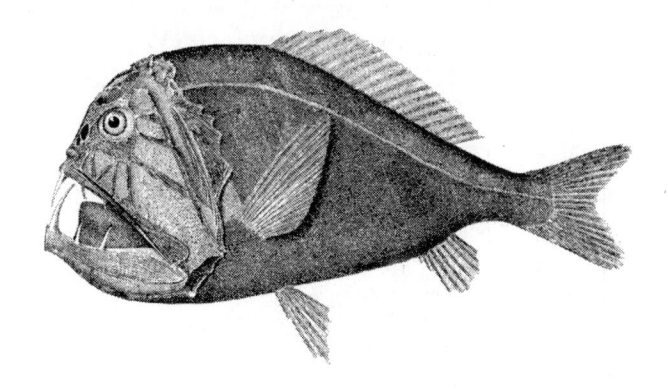

The Fangtooth

Fishermen may also see the Sargassum Fish in the subtropical waters off Florida. The ugly-looking fish blends into the seaweed habitat it likes and has a mottled color. This voracious hunter is also a cannibal that likes to feast on youngsters of its kind. It can make its mouth much larger than normal and can then suck in passing fish, even swallowing fish that are larger than itself. If a larger fish is about to gobble it down, the Sargassum fish can leap above the surface of the water, land on a mat of weed, and survive out of water for some time. (See image above.)

Speaking of fish with fang-like teeth, we need to mention the Viperfish, also found in the sea. Those fierce-looking teeth with a hinged lower jaw make it a formidable hunter that likes to lure its prey with an organ on its dorsal spine that produces a flashing light.

I should also include the Anglerfish with a fleshy growth coming out of its head to lure in prey (see image to the left).

There is also the Hagfish, an eel that likes to produce slime.

And let's not forget the Lamprey or Lamprey Eel, which sometimes attaches itself to larger fish to suck out their blood (see image below).

Lamprey Eel

Anyway, these are some of my suggestions for "Ugly Fish of the Month." I know that some fish are probably ugly in order to ward off other fish.

But I suppose fish of the opposite gender must think they are attractive enough to mate with.

Chapter 19: The Many Fish Species of North Florida's Waters

I actually began thinking of writing on this topic when I was in my favorite overseas city: Istanbul, Turkey. While spending over an hour watching Turkish fishermen reel in an occasional really puny fish near Galata Bridge, I thought about some of the many fish that my friends and I have caught in the rivers and lakes of North Florida.

My favorite has to be the largemouth bass (pictured to the left), which is the state's official freshwater fish. The olive-green beauty with some dark spots along each flank is the largest of the black basses and can reach an overall length of over 29 inches (.7 meters). It can weigh up to about 25 pounds (11 kilograms) and live on average a respectable 16 years.

Maybe the strangest-looking fish in our inland waters is the Florida gar (pictured here). They are not really popular to eat, and their roe can actually be toxic to people and animals. The adults feed on fish, shrimp, and crayfish, while the young ones like insects and other small fish.

The gar can measure in length from 20 to 50 inches (.5 – 1.3 meters) and will usually weight 3 to 9 pounds (1.4 – 4 kilograms). Although one can eat the gar, most people do not. And they sure won't win any beauty contests.

One small, but favorite fish among Florida fishermen is the bluegill, a species with several different names: bream, brim, copper nose, and panfish.

The fish are known for their dorsal fin, forked tail, and little spot at the back of the dorsal fin.

They are usually found in lakes and ponds as they feast on insects and larvae. You can often identify the bluegill by the bright blue edge along their gill rakers (see image to the left).

They're considered pests and therefore are outlawed in places like Germany and Japan, but Florida fishermen like them a lot.

They're somewhat small, ranging from 4 to 12 inches (.1 – .3 meters) in length and weighing up to 4 pounds (1.8 kilograms).

The bluegill are important in preserving the health of our lakes and ponds as they keep crustaceans and insects in check. One fish alone can eat up to six times its own weight in summertime.

Helpful hint to fishermen who want to catch them: use polarized sunglasses to see through the water and find the fish's spawning beds.

Fish Species of North Florida's Waters

Another popular fish is the Florida trout. The state has several species of the fish, including the Spotted Seatrout. In Jacksonville there is a 20-mile-long (32-kilometer-long) Trout River off the St. Johns River.

The photo here is of my son, Brendan, with one of the many trout we caught in the Waccasassa River near Otter Creek in North Florida.

We had a fishing guide with us to find the best fishing spots. I have long depended on such guides for help in finding the keepers. Otherwise I would waste too much time trying to find the best spots for fishing.

The 1975 Florida Legislature adopted the Atlantic sailfish as the state's official saltwater fish.

Ernest Hemingway in Key West, Florida, in the 1940s, with an Atlantic sailfish he had caught

Watery Critters

The importance and fun of fishing our waters have influenced the choice of high school mascots in the state, mascots which include sharks (14 schools), dolphins (3), barracudas (2), stingrays (2), fighting tarpons (1), manta rays (1), marlins (1), etc.

Such schools sometimes have a model of their namesake mascot prominently displayed, as does Miami's Coral Reef High School with its barracuda figure/mascot.

With the state's 3 million acres of ponds, lakes, and reservoirs, as well as some 12,000 miles (19,312 km) of fishable rivers, streams, and canals, it's no wonder that we can rightly claim to be the Fishing Capital of the World. So get out and enjoy our remarkable weather and unbeatable fishing. Be one of the 1.4 million anglers who fish our waterways.

And spread the word about how good the fishing is in North Florida. We should be unselfish enough to let lots of our friends from elsewhere know about this great section of our great state.

Conclusion

This has been a collection of small chapters about North Florida waterways: its rivers, lakes, springs, shipwrecks, and what I call "Watery Critters." Some of the stories were based on several that I had written in a free monthly magazine, *Coastal Angler Magazine*, especially its North Central Florida edition. One can pick up a copy at numerous locations throughout the state or access the online version at this web site: http://coastalanglermag.com/local-editions/.

Bibliography

Boning, Charles R. *Florida's Rivers*. Sarasota, FL: Pineapple Press, 2007.

Gannon, Michael V. *Florida: A Short History*. Gainesville: Univ. Press of Florida, 1993.

McCarthy, Kevin. *St. Johns River Guidebook*. Second edition. Sarasota, FL: Pineapple Press, 2008.

McCarthy, Kevin. *Suwannee River Guidebook*. Sarasota, FL: Pineapple Press, 2009.

McCarthy, Kevin. *Thirty Florida Shipwrecks*. Sarasota, FL: Pineapple Press, 1992.

Milanich, Jerald T. *Florida Indians and the Invasion from Europe*. Gainesville: Univ. Press of Florida, 1995.

Milanich, Jerald T. *Florida's Indians from Ancient Times to the Present*. Gainesville: Univ. Press of Florida, 1998.

Morris, Allen. *Florida Place Names*. Sarasota, FL: Pineapple Press, 1995.

Mueller, Edward A. *St. Johns River Steamboats*. Jacksonville: E.A. Mueller, 1986.

Purdy, Barbara. *The Art and Archaeology of Florida's Wetlands*. Boca Raton, FL: CRC Press, 1991.

Rawlings, Marjorie Kinnan. *Cross Creek*. New York: Scribner, 1942.

Stamm, Doug. *The Springs of Florida*. Sarasota, FL: Pineapple Press, 1994.

Photo Credits

The photos in this book were taken by the author, Kevin McCarthy, unless otherwise noted. Other sources: Cover: Jesse Kunerth - Fotolia.com; title page: Steve Byland; p. i: © Can Stock Photo Inc. / suwanneeredhead; p. 1: Ebyabe; p. 2: Steve Davis; p. 3 (top): Karl Musser, (bottom): Florida State Archives; p. 4 (top): Pfly, (bottom): Karl Musser; p. 5 (top): Karl Musser, (bottom): Mwanner at en.wikipedia; p. 6: Jonathan Zander; p. 8 (top): O.W. Brierly, (bottom): The Athenaeum; p. 9: Library of Congress; p. 10: Michael Slonecker; p. 11 (both): Florida State Archives; p. 12 (top): Florida State Archives; p. 13 (top): U.S. Forest Service; p. 15: (top): Karl Musser, (bottom): Ebyabe; p. 17: Giuseppe Moretti; p. 18: E.P. Christy; p. 25 (top): Pfly; (bottom): Ebyabe; p. 26 (top): Ebyabe, (bottom): Thomsonmg2000; pp. 27-30: Library of Congress; pp. 31-33: Florida State Archives; p. 34: Library of Congress; pp. 35-38: private archives; p. 39: TampaAGS for AGS Media; p. 40: NASA; pp. 41-44: Florida State Archives; pp. 45-48: Ebyabe; pp. 55-56: Florida State Archives; p. 57 (top): Charles R. Knight; p. 57 (bottom) & p. 58 (bottom): Florida State Archives; p. 58 (top): Reynold Brown; pp. 59 & 60: U.S. Navy; p. 61: William Trotter; pp. 62 & 63: Ebyabe; p. 64: Steve Roguski; p. 65: William Trotter; pp. 66,67 (both): Florida State Archives; p. 68: Steve Roguski; p. 69: William Trotter; p. 70 (both): unknown; p. 71: ErgoSum88; p. 72: Steve Roguski; p. 74: AdA Durden; p. 75: jose garcia; p. 76 (top): pix2go, (bottom): EEI_Tony; p. 77 (top): Brian Lasenby; p. 77 (bottom): Steve Byland; p. 78: andyastbury; p. 80: Brian Gratwicke; p. 80 (top): ukanda, (bottom): Bachrach44; p. 81 (top): NOAA FishWatch, (bottom): MoodyGroove at en.wikipedia; p. 82: Harlequeen from Cambridge, United Kingdom; p. 83 (bottom): Engbretson/ U.S. Fish and Wildlife Service; p. 84 (top): Laszloilyes, (bottom): William Buelow Gould; p. 85 (top): G. Brown Goode and Tarleton H. Bean, (bottom): A. H. Baldwin; p. 86 (top): internet, (bottom): Ellen Edmonson and Hugh Chrisp; p. 87 (top): Timothy Knepp, (bottom): nfinitysend at en.wikipedia; p. 88: Eric Engbretson, U.S. Fish and Wildlife Service; p. 89 (bottom): Florida Memory; p. 90: Coral Reef High School.

About the Author

Kevin McCarthy (pictured below at Manatee Springs along the Suwannee River) served for two years in Turkey in the Peace Corps (1963–65) and earned his M.A. in English (1966) and his Ph.D. in Linguistics (1970), both from the Univ. of North Carolina–Chapel Hill.

He taught Linguistics and English at the University of Florida (UF) for 33 years, plus a year in Lebanon as a Fulbright Professor and two years in Saudi Arabia as a Fulbright Professor. The University of Florida named him its Distinguished Alumni Professor before he retired in 2005.

He has twice taught writing workshops in Vietnam and has taught in Spain for part of three summers.

He has had 56 books published, mostly about Florida, as well as over 40 articles in scholarly and popular journals and has given over 300 talks to schools and academic groups. For images of his book covers, see his web site: kevinmccarthy.us.

He can be reached at ceyhankevin@gmail.com

Index

Abbeville, GA, 66
ACF River Basin, 27
"Airport '77," 58
Alabama, 27,30,63
Alapaha River, 15
Alaska, 59,83
America's Cup, 8
American Heritage Rivers, 5
America yacht, 2,7-10
Anglerfish, 86
Annapolis, 10
Apalachicola (town), 26
Apalachicola Bay, 2,27-30
Apalachicola Bluffs, 25
Apalachicola Nat. Forest, 25
Apalachicola River, 1,2,4,25-30,65
Apalachicola Tribe, 25
Archie Carr Nat. Wildlife Refuge, 80
Astatulq, 45
Atlanta, 27
Atlantic Ocean, 3,6,59,60
Atlantic sailfish, 89

Bahama Islands, 43
Baker County, 23
Ball, Ed, 55
Barred owl, 6
Bartram, John, 40
Bartram, William, 2, 40,43
Basilone, 60
Battle of Bloody Marsh, 3
Battle of Ocean Pond, 23
Battle of Olustee, 62
Bering Strait, 55
Bermuda, 8
Big Lake Harris, 46
Blarney Castle, 83
Blue Spring State Park, 5
Bluegill, 88
Boning, Charles, 39
Branford, 65-67
British Colonial Period, 25
Brown Pelican, 77

Caloosahatchee River, 1
Camilla, 8
Cape Canaveral, 79
Caribbean, 59
Carolina Colony, 4
Cedar Key, 22,66
Charleston, SC, 62
Chattahoochee, 3
Chattachoochee River, 4,25,27
Christy, E.P., 18
City of Hawkinsville, 65-68
Civil War, 8,9,12,22. 23,32,61-64,66
Clay County, 44
Clays Landing, 66

Coastal Angler Magazine, 73,91
Coleridge, Samuel T., 2
Columbus (ghost town), 2,21-24,65
Commodore, 69-72
Commodore's Point, 70
Confederacy, 8
Coral Reef High School, 90
Cormorants, 75
Crane, Stephen, 69-72
Crawfordville, 55
"Creature from the Black Lagoon," 58
Crescent City, 11
Crescent Lake, 7,35
Cuba, 43,69,70,72

Daytona Beach, 37, 69,70
Dead Rivers, 1
DeLeon Springs, 44
Dept. of Justice, 63
Dixie County, 33,50, 68
Drayton Island, 11
Drew, George, 21
Dunns Creek, 7-10,35
DuPont, Alfred, 55

Eagles, 78
East Florida, 2,25
Eastside High School, 42
Edward Ball Wakulla Springs St. Park, 55

94

Ellaville, 21
England, 7
Everglades, 41,73,74

Fangtooth Fish, 85
Fargo, Georgia, 15
Ferries, 11-14,31-34
Fl. Dept. of Agriculture & Cons. Services, 29
Fl. Dept. of State, 68
Flathead Catfish, 83
Flint River, 4,25,27
Florida Aquifer, 50
Florida gar, 87
Florida LAKEWATCH, 41
"Florida, My Florida," 18
Florida Panhandle, 25,27,55,59,83
Florida State Archives, 35
Florida State Legislature, 18,19,41,89
Florida State University, 57
"Florida, Where the Sawgrass Meets the Sky," 19
Fort Fanning, 32
Fort Gates Ferry, 2, 11-14
Foster, Stephen, 2,17-20
Franklin County, 26, 29
Free Ferry, 33
Fruitland, 11

Gainesville, 42
Galata Bridge, 87
George III, King, 40
Georgia, 3,4,15,25, 27,30,43,54
Germany, 88
Ghost towns, 21-24
Gilchrist County, 33, 51
Gornto Springs, 50
Gorrie, Dr. John, 26
Great Britain, 40
Great Egrets, 74,77
Green Heron, 75,76
Grey Building, 56
Guaranto Springs, 50
Gulf of Mexico, 3,4, 15,22,25-30,43,55
Gulf Transportation Co., 66

Hagfish, 86
Halifax River, 36,37
Harris Chain (of lakes), 46
Harris, Ebenezer, 45
Harris, Frank, 45
Hart Springs, 51-54
Hawkinsville Deepwater Boat Lines, 66
Hemingway, Ernest, 89
Hillsborough River, 1
Holland, Keith, 63
Hontoon Island, 11
Howard T. Odum Fl. Springs Institute, 50

Ice Age, 56
Ichetucknee River, 2
Indian River County, 5
Internat. Union for the Cons. of Nature, 81
Ireland, 83
Isle of Wight, 8
Istanbul, Turkey, 87

Jacksonville, 6,9, 62,63,70,71
Jacksonville University, 72
Japan, 88
"Joe Panther," 58

Key West, 22,89
Kingston, Ontario, 62
Knight, Robert, 50
"Kubla Khan" (poem), 2

Lake Apopka, 47,48
Lake County, 39,45
Lake Eustis, 45
Lake George, 39,40
Lake Harris, 45-48
Lake Michigan, 40
Lake Okeechobee, 40
Lake Seminole, 3,4
Lamprey Eel, 86
Largemouth bass, 87
Levy County, 29
Library of Congress, 34
Live Oak, 21
Lizardfish, 84
Loggerhead Turtles, 79-82

Mammoths, 1
Manatee Springs, 49
Manatees, 5
Mandarin, 64
Mandarin Point, 63
Maple Leaf, 61-64
Marion County, 34
Martin, Robert, 32
Mastodons, 1,56,57
Mayport, 6,11,70
McCarthy, Brendan, 89
McCaskill, Michael, 67
Melbourne Beach, 80
Memphis, 8,9
Miami, 18,42
Miami River, 1
Mississippi, 17
Mississippi River, 4
Mobile, 26
Mobile Bay, 4
Moretti, Giuseppe, 17
Morris, Allen, 45
Mosquito Inlet, 70
Museum of Florida History, 56

Nassau, 8
National Archives, 63
National Historic Landmark, 63
National Natural Landmark, 58
National Register of Hist. Places, 58
National Weather Service, 54
Native Americans, 1, 6,16,25
Naval Station Mayport, 6
New York Yacht Club, 7
Newman, Paul, 13
Newnan, Daniel, 43
Newnans Lake, 41-43
New Orleans, 22,26
"Night Moves," 58

Ocala, 34
Ocala National Forest, 11
Ocklawaha River, 34,36
Odum, Howard, 50
Okeehumkee, 36
Okefenokee Swamp, 3,15,54
"Old Folks at Home," 17-20
Old Town, 66-68
Olustee, 23
Oman, 79
"The Open Boat," 71
Oriskany, 59
Orlando, 45
Ormond, 38
Ormond Beach, 37,72
Otter Creek, 89
Oysters, 27-30

Paelo-Indians, 55
Palatka, 7,13,34, 35,62
Palatlakaha River, 45
Pearl River, 4
Pee Dee River, 17
Pensacola, 59
Perdido River, 3,4
Philadelphia, 70
Pithlachocco, 43
Pittsburgh, Penn., 17
Pleistocene Epoch, 55
Ponce de Leon Inlet, 70
Ponce de Leon Lighthouse, 71
Port of Tampa, 67
Putnam County, 13

Reconstruction, 21
Red Badge of Courage, 69
Red Irish Lord (fish), 83
Roberts, J.R., 32
Roberts, Kate, 32
Rock Bluff Ferry, 33
Royal Yacht Squadron 100 Guin. Cup, 7

Santa Fe River, 15

Sargassum fish, 85
Savannah River, 3
Sebastian Inlet, 79
Seminole Indian Wars, 45
Seminoles, 16,41-43
Sharpie sailboats, 12
Shipwrecks, 59-72
Silver River, 34
Silver Springs, 34
Slavery, 19
South Carolina, 3,17,62
Spain, 3,4,31,69,72
Spotted Seatrout, 89
Springs, 49-58
St. Augustine, 60
St. George Sound, 27
St. Joe Company, 55
St. Johns River, 1,2,5-9,11-14,34-36,39,61-64,70,89
St. Marks River, 2,55
St. Marys River, 3
St. Simon's Island, 3
St. Vincent Sound, 27
Stamm, Doug, 49
Stargazer, 84
Steamboats, 3,22,36,65-68
Stephen Foster Folk Cul. Center State Park, 19
Suwannee River, 1,2,15-24,31-33,43,51-54,57,65-68
Suwannee River State Park, 21,24,65
Suwannee River Water Man. District, 52,54
Suwannee River Wilderness Trail, 51
"The Swanee River," 17,18

Tallahassee, 2,35,55,56
Tarzan movies, 58
"Tarzan's New York Adventure," 58
Tates Hell State Forest, 25
Three States (steamboat), 67
Timucua, 16
Tomoka Landing, 38
Tomoka River, 36,37
Too Wendy, 12
Torreya State Park, 1,25
Tri-colored Heron, 75,76
Trout River, 89
Turtle excluder devices, 81

U.S. Envir. Prot. Agency, 5
U.S. Naval Academy, 10
U.S. Navy, 59,60
University of Florida, 73,80

Victoria, Queen, 8
Viperfish, 86
Vista, 66
Volusia Blue Spring, 50
Volusia County, 36,39,44

Wabasso Beach, 80
Waccasassa River, 89
Wakulla County, 29
Wakulla River, 55
Wakulla Springs, 55-58
War of 1812, 4
"Way Down Upon the Suwannee River," 17
Weissmuller, Johnny, 58
Wekiva River, 6
West Florida, 2,4,25
White Egrets, 75
White Springs, 16,19,50
White-water rapids, 16
Wilcox Landing, 32
Withlacoochee River, 15,21
World Turtle Day, 79
World War II, 60
Worthington Springs, 50

Yalaha, 45
Yazoo River, 17
Yearty, Thomas, 66